# Dogs Do The Silliest Things

# Dogs Do The Silliest Things

## Alexandra Ortolja-Baird

BARRON'S

# THIS BOOK IS DEDICATED TO D'ARTAGNAN

First edition for North America, published in
2004 by Barron's Educational Series, Inc.

All inquiries should be addressed to:
Barron's Educational Series, Inc.
250 Wireless Boulevard
Hauppauge, NY 11788
http://www.barronseduc.com

Library of Congress Catalog Card Number 2004103215

International Standard Book Number 0-7641-5805-8

Published by MQ Publications Limited
12 The Ivories, 6-8 Northampton Street
London N1 2HY

Printed and bound in China

9 8 7 6 5 4 3 2 1

A Canadian psychologist is selling a video that teaches you how to test your dog's IQ. Here's how it works: if you spend $12.99 for the video, your dog is smarter than you.

JAY LENO

6

Oh, what is the matter with poor Puggy-Wug? Pet him and kiss him and give him a hug. Run and fetch him a suitable drug. Wrap him up tenderly all in a rug. That is the way to cure Puggy-Wug.

WINSTON CHURCHILL

# Every boy should have two things: a dog, and a mother willing to let him have one.

ANONYMOUS

10

We've begun to long for the pitter-patter of little feet—so we bought a dog. Well, it's cheaper, and you get more feet.

RITA RUDNER

13

I was born in front of a camera and really don't know anything else.

14

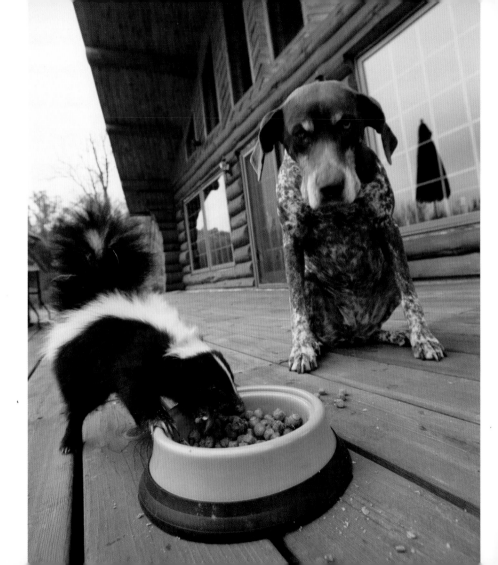

# Never trust a dog to watch your food.

PATRICK, AGE 10

17

Yesterday I was a dog. Today I'm a dog. Tomorrow I'll probably still be a dog. Sigh! There's so little hope for advancement.

SNOOPY

# Win together, lose together, play together, stay together.

DEBRA MANCUSO

# A door is what a dog is perpetually on the wrong side of.

**Ogden Nash**

"Grandmother, what big eyes you have!" said Little Red Riding Hood.

"All the better to see you with, my dear!"

BROTHERS GRIMM

When in doubt, make a fool of yourself. There is a microscopically thin line between being brilliantly creative and acting like the most gigantic idiot on earth. So what the hell, leap.

CYNTHIA HEIMEL

**No one appreciates the very special genius of your conversation as much as the dog does.**

CHRISTOPHER MORLEY

# Stop worrying about the potholes in the road and enjoy the journey.

Babs Hoffman

If you are a dog and your owner suggests that you wear a sweater, suggest that he wear a tail.

FRAN LEBOWITZ

33

I bought a dog the other day…I named him Stay. It's fun to call him…"Come here, Stay! Come here, Stay!" He went insane. Now he just ignores me and keeps on typing.

STEVEN WRIGHT

Whatever is the natural propensity of a person is hard to overcome. If a dog were made a king, he would still gnaw at his shoelaces.

HITOPADESA

# I've had a wonderful time, but this wasn't it.

GROUCHO MARX

38

**Effort only fully releases its reward after a person refuses to quit.**

NAPOLEON HILL

41

# There is no psychiatrist in the world like a puppy licking your face.

BERN WILLIAMS

When you jump for joy,
beware that no one
moves the ground from
beneath your feet.

Stanislaw J. Lec

I am happy I have competition. It keeps me on my toes all the while and stops me from becoming complacent. So, it works to my advantage.

AMISHA PATEL

# Every mile is two in winter.

GEORGE HERBERT

We got our lungs from Daddy, and we exercised them early and often during those years...when that famous McEntire yell saved our hides more than once.

REBA McENTIRE

A little madness in
the Spring
Is wholesome even
for the King.

EMILY DICKINSON

# Silence is one great art of conversation.

ANONYMOUS

I never set out to be weird. It was always the other people who called me weird.

FRANK ZAPPA

# Insanity: doing the same thing over and over again and expecting different results.

ALBERT EINSTEIN

# Enthusiasm is the leaping lightning, not to be measured by the horsepower of understanding.

RALPH WALDO EMERSON

# Life is what you make it: if you snooze, you lose; and if you snore, you lose more.

**PHYLLIS GEORGE**

Everyday happiness means getting up in the morning, and you can't wait to finish your breakfast...You can't wait to get out—and you can't wait to come home, because the soup is hot.

GEORGE BURNS

65

# Some days you're the dog—some days you're the hydrant.

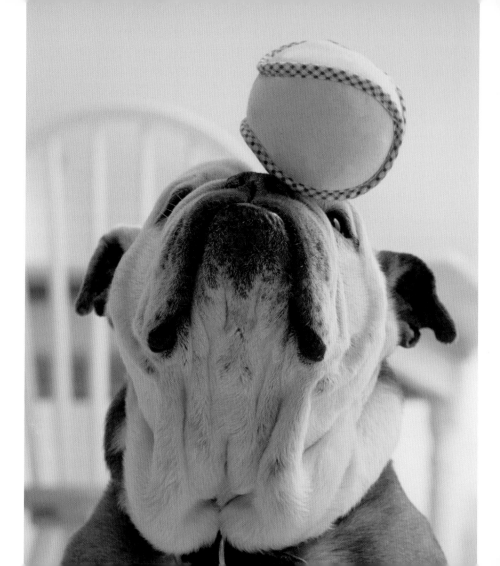

If there is anything that a man can do well, I say let him do it. Give him a chance.

ABRAHAM LINCOLN

Call it a clan,
call it a network,
call it a tribe,
call it a family.
Whatever you
call it, whoever
you are, you
need one.

JANE HOWARD

The reason a dog has so many friends is that he wags his tail instead of his tongue.

ANONYMOUS

73

# If you think dogs can't count, try putting three dog biscuits in your pocket and then giving Fido only two of them.

PHIL PASTORET

# Happiness is a ball after which we run wherever it rolls, and we push it with our feet when it stops.

JOHANN WOLFGANG VON GOETHE

Jump into the middle of things, get your hands dirty, fall flat on your face, and then reach for the stars.

BEN STEIN

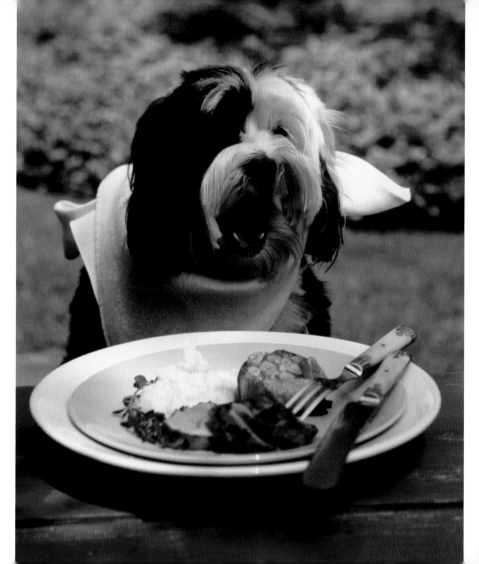

# My favorite animal is steak.

FRAN LEBOWITZ

# Outside of a dog, a book is man's best friend. Inside of a dog, it's too dark to read.

GROUCHO MARX

An intellectual snob is someone who can listen to the William Tell Overture and not think of The Lone Ranger.

DAN RATHER

# Every dog must have its day.

Jonathan Swift

# Sanity calms, but madness is more interesting.

JOHN RUSSELL

I have a great dog.
She's half Lab, half
pit bull. A good
combination. Sure,
she might bite off
my leg, but she'll
bring it back to me.

Jimi Celeste

I wish my hair was thicker, and I wish my feet were prettier. My toes are really ugly. I wish my ears were smaller. And my nose could be smaller too.

BRITNEY SPEARS

# ...an' sometimes there's no sugar an' sometimes there's no root beer. But there's always soap!

DENNIS THE MENACE

94

# Photo Credits

# Text Credits